CODE OF CLOTHES

A Modern Guide to Catapult Your
Confidence, Credibility and Career

Elizabeth T. Jones

Code of Clothes

A Modern Guide to Catapult Your Confidence, Credibility and Career

Elizabeth T. Jones

Printed in the USA

ISBN 978-1-7341278-0-5

Cover Design, Layout and Graphics by Jim Fenster Design
www.jimfensterdesign.com

Code of Clothes LLC
www.codeofclothes.com
Elizabeth.jones@codeofclothes.com

Introduction

Code of Clothes was borne out of my passionate belief that personal appearance expresses credibility, creativity and commitment in the workplace.

A person's visual appearance is a significant non-verbal communication that can build respect, trust and confidence.

- Gone are the days of traditional business dress codes. Today's corporate workplace dress codes are less defined and less formulaic than twenty years ago.

- Employees want flexibility and independence and do not want to be told what to wear to work. With this flexibility exists the potential to positively differentiate oneself or, conversely, to gain negative attention.

- Personal presentation is viewed as off-limits, superficial and irrelevant within the workplace. It is an overlooked skill that can be developed to significantly improve confidence and credibility and to propel a career.

- This guide will: (1) explain the power of your personal image, (2) demonstrate the impact of personal presentation on an individual's credibility and confidence, and (3) provide tips and tools on how to easily improve one's own professional image.

I firmly believe in the confidence and power that comes from wearing a fabulous new pair of heels, the latest vegan leather pants, that classic 10 year-old navy blazer, or a fun pair of vintage glasses. I have seen the power of clothes work for entry level associates all the way up to CEOs.

I hope you find this guide valuable as you enter the workforce, start your own business or pursue any professional passion.

Table of Contents

Reality 1: First Impressions Count

Non-verbal communication is extremely important with regard to first impressions. Some psychologists estimate that non-verbal communication is four times as effective as verbal communication or actions.

What do you notice when walking into a meeting, a conference, or an interview?

You notice a person's appearance.

While you may not consciously realize you are noticing a person's clothes, hair or shoes, you interpret a person's overall presentation prior to anything that person says.

Within the first few seconds of meeting someone, your brain is quickly and subconsciously processing many things about a person.

Specifically within a work environment, you are quickly determining a person's:

- Credibility
- Culture fit
- Commitment
- Energy level
- Seniority

Your response and assessment are very powerful and can shape how you view the person's performance and potential.

Personal presentation is an easy way to communicate important attributes about yourself, while setting the tone for your environment.

SUPER short time to impress

The window for creating a memorable first impression upon meeting someone is approximately seven seconds. Therefore, you must act very quickly to make a strong and positive first impression. This seven second window may seem a bit extreme, but your mind is not as rational or objective as you think it should be in professional situations.

Looking credible, respectable and intelligent via your professional attire is a significant part of the psychology of making a memorable impression. It is just as important as other non-verbal cues such as smiling, making eye contact, and verbal responses.

Over 95% of communication occurs via non-verbal communications.

*"There is no such thing as non-communication because the non-verbal is always there" * Charles Galloway, an expert in non-verbal communication.*

Your attire supports critical characteristics that ultimately result in making the sale, convincing the client, getting the job or being promoted.

Credibility:

- you are displaying that you can be trusted and professional
- you are verifying the level of performance that you are willing to give the other person, project or team
- you can offset challenges in your experience by showcasing your professional presentation

Culture fit:

- you are displaying that you are aware of what is necessary to succeed in the organization
- you are displaying that you have done your research on the company, client or project
- you are showing that you are an excellent fit for the organization

Commitment & Energy:

- you are showing respect for the specific project and for yourself
- you are communicating that this project and your team are important
- you are communicating that others should do the same

Seniority:

- you are communicating that you are the leader of the project
- you are indicating that you WANT to be the leader of the team or the organization

Real world examples of how first impressions are created intentionally and unintentionally.

Intentional

Interviewing is literally all about first impressions.

Miles was a young, bright candidate with an impressive resume that most employers would find appealing.   He was interviewing for his first full-time position after earning both a BA and an MBA. He was particularly interested in this large marketing company because of their new hip culture and their stated interest in non-traditional marketing strategies that targeted a twenty-something demographic.

The marketing managers assigned to interview Miles knew that the company—and specifically the team—needed talented, smart young employees to help them better connect with their consumers and help transform the internal culture.

Miles made it through multiple rounds of interviews at the company because he exceeded the candidate criteria. However, there were a few common topics that surfaced in the interview debriefs.

No one debated that Miles was smart and motivated. This was evidenced by his resume and his answers to questions.

The one main concern marketing managers had centered around Miles' apparent nervousness in interviews. They worried whether these "nerves" would interfere in his ability to connect with team members. He had trouble making eye contact, did not seem to smile except at the end of each interview, and his non-verbal cues were distracting to two of the interviewers.
Two managers assumed that Miles was just shy, while the other two managers thought that his "nerves" disqualified

him from the position.

The other topic that bubbled up during the debrief was his interview attire—in a very positive way. He arrived for every round of interviews looking very professional, fun and polished, with a few sophisticated accessories—exactly what this company was wanting to infuse into their culture, workforce and products. The team was impressed by his sophisticated presentation and keen awareness of their trendy culture.

Ultimately, the team decided to extend Miles an offer, since he embodied all the characteristics that this company was eagerly wanting to acquire—he was trendy, smart, creative and professional. The team determined that they could help develop Miles' non-verbal skills over time.

Miles' inherent understanding of the corporate culture and his ability to show this understanding through his attire created positive first impressions and balanced out his challenges, resulting in a job offer.

This is the power of clothes.

Unintentional

Public speaking: first impressions of a different kind.

First impressions are not just reserved for job interviews. As people are promoted to new roles with increased responsibilities, they have opportunities to create new impressions. Many companies have annual leadership conferences that showcase presentations by top executives and their respective internal teams make up the audience.

At one international corporate event, one of the main speakers was a newly promoted Vice President of marketing, communication and sales.

Vanessa was smart, confident and well-liked in her previous positions. Her new role tripled her direct reports, and she now directed multiple teams and clients. She was spending the bulk of her time presenting in front of many groups within the company.

With this new promotion to VP, Vanessa assumed a new sense of executive "style" that she thought she needed as she transitioned to a more prominent figure within the company. Her transition was a dramatic shift. Vanessa was intending to communicate confidence and boldness; however, this new look registered as surprising and distracting.

During this leadership conference, Vanessa was making a presentation about her role and the future of her teams. This global conference was the largest display of her new style. After her presentation, many people informally noted and commented on this new style but not in a positive way.

Her new style was surprisingly brash and contrasted with the corporate reputation that she had built up over the past few years. Instead of taking her more seriously, discussing the projects that she presented, and getting excited about this new leader, associates were distracted by her new look.

This chatter is unfair, immature and counter-productive; yet this is also human nature. People judge others and have expectations associated with their leaders.

The unfortunate part of this situation is that Vanessa was intentionally trying to make a positive change that reflected her excitement, yet it backfired and undermined her credibility.

This is the power of clothes.

TAKE ACTION:

Evaluate:

- What is your go-to outfit to make a positive impression?
- Does this communicate what you want?
- What part indicates credibility?
- What part indicates a good cultural fit?

Determine:

- What would you do to refresh this outfit?
- Do you have current alternatives?
- Does your wardrobe allow for flexibility?
- What is your budget for refreshing your work attire?

Create:

- The outfit you would wear for a meeting with the CEO of your company.
- Multiple ideal outfits for key presentations and interviews.

Reality 2: You Are Your Own Brand

You are your own brand.

Your everyday work "uniform" shows your lifestyle choices, your priorities and your attention to detail. Your managers and colleagues judge you every day, both positively and negatively based on your appearance.

Judging may seem harsh and dramatic, but managers and colleagues are continually monitoring your performance and part of this is your personal presentation, not just your power point presentations.

Everyone believes that managers only assess you on your work performance not appearance. Wrong. They assess you on both aspects - one is just more explicit than the other.

Evaluating people on their appearance is part of being humans and what fuels a multitude of billion-dollar industries, like fashion, beauty and advertising. This judgment is not always overt, especially in a professional setting. It is something that we subconsciously do on a daily basis.

You may believe that evaluating a person's professional appearance does not occur because...

- no one says anything
- there is not a formal dress code policy
- how you look is irrelevant to your job

However, people in a work environment will NOT say:

"Wow looks like you had a rough night!"

"Did you sleep in those clothes?"

"Did you get dressed in the dark?"

"Is that jacket two sizes too small?"

"Why are you wearing a suit & tie in a casual workplace?"

"Is that your dad's shirt?"

"Could you clean up your toenails before wearing those sandals?"

These are impolite, insensitive and inappropriate comments to say to a colleague.

On the flip side, it may be rare to share positive feedback about one's appearances too, such as:

"That's an awesome dress"

"You look like you're going to rock this presentation"

"You always look so fun & trendy"

"Great loafers, dude"

Commenting on personal style and appearance is challenging. Most people are concerned that their comments could be misinterpreted as an insult or as a sexual innuendo, especially if coming from a colleague or superior of a different gender.

During my research, multiple managers in varying industries stated without hesitation that they notice what their associates are wearing and how they present themselves. They consider this aspect to be a fair and important part of an associate's potential for advancement in the company. However, none of the managers said that they shared this feedback, positive or negative, with their direct reports.

The reality is that everyone is assessing you on how you appear, consciously and unconsciously. This is a cumulative judgment that is aggregated from daily interactions. This judgment may not be formally documented, but it is integrated and assessed as part of your potential and overall professionalism.

Rather than getting stressed out about this judgment, get motivated to promote yourself through your attire.

This is a powerful mindset that is as relevant to an entrepreneur launching a new business as it is to someone in a large corporation.

All day, every day, what you wear to work counts...

Real World example:

After graduating from business school, I worked in New York City in the beauty industry. One of the top creative designers was a woman in her mid-fifties who had been working in advertising, publishing and marketing for years.

In New York City, it is typical to wear a predominance of black. What is unusual is going to the extreme of wearing 100% black, every day, all year long, without the smallest hint of any other color.

This woman wore all black every day, all year long, regardless of the season, occasion, or meeting. She created her own professional uniform and was very intentional about this look. She made a very calculated professional decision that would subtly call attention to herself while simultaneously deferring attention to her work.

She knew that she would be judged by what she was wearing, given the industry and market that she worked within every day. Yet, she wanted to limit the judgements of her personal appearance to only a few options, such as:

- *"that's very artsy"*
- *"very NYC"*
- *"typical creative-type"*

She knew her colleagues would quickly grow accustomed to her all-black uniform. Plus, the intentionality of wearing an all-black uniform every day functioned subtly in a few other significant ways:

- by deflecting attention to her creative and professional work, rather than to a personal style;
- by suggesting she was so focused on her work that she does not waste time on herself;
- by allowing her to maintain sophistication and credibility everyday; and
- by allowing her to feel confident everyday

This intentionality was part of her own brand and her own persona, and it was how she differentiated herself from the other executives in the company. She found this empowering and a key to her success.

This is the power of clothes.

Action:

Be aware about what you are communicating non-verbally via your personal appearance.

Assess:

- What are you communicating with your current appearance?
- What do the managers two or three levels above you communicate with their appearance?

Determine:

- Is this what I want to communicate?
- What do I want to represent?

Create:

- Three new outfits that visually represent what you believe is necessary to succeed in your company.

v

Reality 3: Clothes Influence Performance

Professional attire is the modern-day armor in today's workplace warfare. It helps signify authority, success and a readiness for workday "battle."

Think, for example, about a physician's white lab coat, a judge's robe, military fatigues, a chef's hat. These are all visual cues of power, credibility and culture.

This battle analogy is a bit dramatic, of course, considering most workplaces are not outwardly confrontational or militaristic. You must be prepared to perform in a way that ensures continued success and be ready for whatever comes across the field or your desk.

Dressing up equals success, yet dressing up means different attire for different industries on different days.

Research suggests that biological changes occur when we get dressed up, such as an increase in heart rate and hormone levels.

Other research has noted that those who want to increase their focus should dress like doctors. In research published in July 2012 in the *Journal of Experimental Social Psychology*, subjects made half as many mistakes on attention-demanding tasks when wearing a white lab coat, which is seen as a sign of power and authority.

Dressing up within the workplace is believed to make people feel more powerful. In a research test in August 2015 in *Social Psychological and Personality Science*, when wearing formal business attire, subjects scored higher on abstract thinking cognitive tests than they did when wearing casual clothes. Abstract cognitive thinking is a key component of creativity and strategy.

"Dressing your best" translates into your best work

Increasing your performance in the workplace does not mean wearing a white lab coat or even a suit every day. In many industries and environments, dressing too formally makes a person irrelevant, outdated and misaligned with the office culture. Knowing your company's culture is vital in determining what level of formality will elevate a person's credibility.

Traditional business attire in today's workplace is quickly becoming outdated, and it has been replaced with more casual and often vague dress codes. (We will discuss dress codes more depth later on.)

Dressing your best is knowing YOUR environment

Your environment and corporate culture will dictate what it means to "dress up."

Action:

Determine several things:

- What is the official HR policy dress code?
- What does the CEO wear? Does this differ from day to day?
- What does your manager wear day to day and on special occasions?
- Do all departments dress at the same level?
- Who are the company's customers? What is their typical dress?
- Do you meet with these customers face to face?
- Do you work remotely?
- Do you travel frequently?

The answers to all these situations have implications for your professional attire and will determine the definition of "dressing up" in your individual environment.

In the Office

Everyone thinks navigating the office look is easy. Look around and see what your team is wearing. Suit? No suit? Jeans? No jeans?

The challenge is determining what is valued in your team and within the company, then reflecting those core values with your professional appearance. This can be accomplished by knowing the right days to wear the right outfits, and by being consistent day to day over a significant period of time.

Example 1

Industry: Manufacturing

Position: Controller

Goal appearance: Most conservatively dressed in the office

Rationale: The controller's credibility is built on accuracy and attention to detail. These values need to be communicated and reflected daily via personal appearance.

Example 2

Industry: Creative Design Agency

Position: Graphic Designer

Goal appearance: Trendy yet polished

Rationale: The designer's credibility is determined by his or her ability to translate a business objective into a creative device. This creative position allows a casual and trendy freedom with personal appearance.

Out of the Office

A person's work attire can be a critical factor in improving your performance when in situations outside headquarters.

Situation 1:

Working from home:

Many people think home is the best workplace environment. "No one will see me, so it does not matter what I look like it or what I'm wearing." This may be accurate for many people who are able to focus despite wearing fleece unicorn pjs.

However, people who work from home often change out of pajamas or sweatpants, and they may even get formally dressed, even when they are not going to be seeing anyone.

This physical change triggers a mental mindset that requires seriousness and boosts performance.

Situation 2:

Presenting in a large or new audience:

Many people use this opportunity to don a new look, thinking they should look special for a special situation. This is a challenging situation, as it can be risky, and it may backfire if they are not 100% sure of their "new" look.

The focus of a presentation in front of a new or large audience needs to be on the content of the presentation, not on the presenter.

The presenter's role is to complement the presentation and add integrity to the content as a subject-matter expert. The objective is NOT to be a distraction from the presentation.

Tailored, subtle and consistent with corporate culture should be the goals of optimal presentation attire.

An awesome outfit can make a presenter feel confident while communicating credibility and authority.

Situation 3:

Traveling:

Work travel presents an interesting situation for many people. Some people simply follow the dress code of their office environment, while some take this opportunity to deviate from the norm by being too casual or too formal. This is the time that knowing the corporate culture is crucial.

Casual dress while traveling may be acceptable, as long as casual does not equal sloppy. You are representing your company, your team and your client. If traveling with colleagues, they are often seeing you in a different environment, yet all the same professional expectations still exist.

Many companies and clothing lines have been responding to these situations by developing fabrics and lines that withstand temperature changes and are "travel" friendly. The benefit is that a person can look professional and still be comfortable.

Real World example:

Today's work environment is continually evolving. For millions of people, this means working from a home office or tele-commuting.

Nancy is a national sales consultant for a growing technology company and she primarily works from her home office. She conducts most of her business on the phone and on her computer with her clients. She is very successful in competing in this fast-paced industry.

Although Nancy works from home, she is very intentional about what she wears each day. Her attire mirrors her day, as if she were in her physical HQ office.

For example, if she is going to be on conference calls or video conferences, she dresses in a business casual outfit. Typically, this is comprised of black pants or jeans, a silk blouse, makeup and shoes. She notes that she transitions into "work" mode by physically getting ready with her outfit, even though she is in her home office.

If she is having a "heads down" day in which she will be working exclusively on her own without interacting with clients or business partners, she dresses down and wears a more casual outfit.

Dressing up for her day benefits Nancy by:

- helping her focus on the goals of the day
- keeping her connected with the culture of the company

Nancy enjoys the benefit of working from home, but she is aware of its disadvantages. The drawbacks include the lack of visibility in the office and a disconnect with colleagues. Nancy goes into the office about every six weeks and is deliberate about how she presents herself while in the casual office.

Due to the uber-casual office culture, she realizes that she could wear almost anything. However, she does not always want to blend in—she wants to be noticed in a positive way.

Typically, she will wear jeans and a jacket or blazer and trendy shoes. She is careful not to be overly dressed up, since that will get her noticed in a negative way. Nancy notes that keeping up with fashion trends takes effort on her part, but it pays dividends in the long run by giving her confidence and credibility.

Trending "up" for the office benefits Nancy by:

- keeping her relevant with her younger colleagues
- communicating leadership and credibility
- energizing her within all of her face-to-face interactions

Nancy said she is always surprised and pleased at how people comment on her accessories or great shoes. This builds her confidence and her credibility.

This is the power of clothes.

Reality 4: Let's Talk Dress Code

The corporate "dress code" in the 1980s, 1990s, and early 2000s was easy. It dictated professional attire for everyone. Everyone wore a suit, regardless of level, gender or industry. There wasn't a lot of room for error, but there wasn't much room for creativity, either. Many corporations had rigid dress codes, and the expectations were clearly outlined in human resource policy handbooks.

There has been a major shift in the past decade with regard to corporate dress codes, as many businesses assess what is necessary, appealing and critical to recruit and retain talent. Corporations have refreshed their corporate image to appeal to a younger generation of recruits and to give incentives to existing employees.

One of the ways to attract a younger demographic was to shift from a formal, traditional professional dress code to a dress code that allowed more personal freedom and creativity. Thus, the onset of "casual Friday", which morphed into "business casual" and then into "jeans Friday." Now, jeans are automatically considered part of the daily dress code in many corporations.

The evolution of the dress code was viewed as an easy and inexpensive way to accomplish many objectives:

- attracting new and younger recruits
- delighting current employees
- encouraging personal creativity
- promoting self-confidence
- aligning with a corporate mission and vision

Along with these benefits, there are challenges that corporations face with the onset of less-structured dress codes:

- Casual is interpreted differently from one person to another, one team to another and one company to another
- Creative dressing can be distracting in the workplace rather than empowering
- It becomes more challenging to determine the hierarchy on each team
- It can be more difficult for some employees to determine how to dress for their own success
- It may be tougher to determine virtual office attire

In order to appropriately present yourself in today's workplace, you need to understand the nuances of various dress codes. This is the tricky part, as there are many different dress codes, and many of these standards are subjective.

A modern list of the ambiguous, subjective and often misunderstood corporate "dress codes"

Business Professional	Industry Ex.	Notes
Suit or jacket, closed-toe dress shoes (women); suit with tie and dress shoes (men)	Banking, Finance, Law	Business professional companies typically are overt about dress code requirements.

Business Casual		
Dressy pants, skirt, blouse, jacket; dress shoes — no jeans Suit, no tie; sport coat, dress shirt, dress shoes—no jeans	Consulting, Marketing, Academics	Some companies are more business than casual, while others are more casual than business

Casual		
Almost anything goes—jeans, pants, polo shirts, short sleeves	Technology, Academics, Manufacturing	Stay away from ripped clothing, shorts (tank tops for men), and anything you would wear to clean out the garage

Smart Casual		
Trendier casual clothes; jeans, cropped pants, boots, open-toed shoes	Creative, Design, Technology, Agencies	Fashion forward looks are great, but stay away from sexy, nighttime looks. No ripped jeans or skin-baring clothes

Jeans Casual		
Same as casual		Regardless if this is all work week or just Fridays; stay away from ripped, dirty or ill-fitting jeans

Travel Casual		
Easy to wear and comfortable clothes	Sales, Consulting, special occasions	Travel attire does not mean sloppy, athletic or bedtime attire; it simply allows for more comfortable options than typical business casual; ie. leisure shoes are ok with casual clothes

Dress for your Day		
Requires each person to determine who they are meeting that day, what they are doing and where	Sales, Consulting, Service Agencies	Each employee should own everything, from a suit, to nice jeans

Dress like you would dress for your Grandmother		
This is the equivalent to casual yet can vary from department to department	Technology firms, Design and Marketing Agencies	This is super subjective and leaves a lot of room for error; this should be interpreted as smart/casual

Real World example:

"All style, no substance"

At a hip urban marketing agency, Mark was a Senior Vice President. He was quick-witted, energetic, confident, and he always assembled good teams to work for him. Most of all, he dressed very well for every occasion. He always knew the right level at which to dress—not too formal, not too casual, and a little trendy—and he always remained poised. He carried himself with confidence and continually looked professional. One assumed that since he presented himself with such competence and charisma, that he performed at a similar level.

The interesting aspect is that Mark did not have a lot of substance behind the professional veneer. He was consistent enough to get the position, but he relied heavily on his supporting teams to meet deadlines and to complete required deliverables. This lack of substance took a long time to manifest itself, since he presented himself with an unwavering, professional appearance, and he made sure to surround himself with credible, hard-working teams.

Mark kept his high-profile positions for as long as he did at all his companies due to his professional appearance and charisma. People wanted him to represent their business, and they assumed he was as credible as he appeared. He was savvy enough to know that he only had a finite time at each company before people would determine his incompetence. He used these transitions to promote himself to the next level at a new company.

Mark cleverly knew the power of clothes.

Business casual for YOU, business professional for ME

In many corporations, the official dress code is business casual or just casual. The one dynamic that occurs over and over is that there seem to be different dress codes depending on your level.

Often, senior leaders do not adhere to the very dress code policy that they approved. They dress more formally than the rest of the company, sometimes wearing a suit when others wear jeans. In many companies, the CEO and the few executive committee members dress far more formally than their teams, the official dress policy or the rest of the company.

They do this: (1) to differentiate themselves as leaders, (2) to signify a level of responsibility and credibility in the company, (3) to show their "old school" culture, and/or (4) out of habit. They know they are the ultimate decision-makers, and they believe either consciously or unconsciously that this level of accountability deserves a more formal presence.

What these leaders do not realize is that they are creating a dichotomy within the company between those who want to follow the approved dress code and those who want to respect the corporate leadership. The complexity and awkwardness arise for those associates who are aware of this dichotomy, and they are unsure what is the "real" dress code.

The question now becomes...

Do you follow the corporate dress code, or do you follow the corporate leaders?

Answer: both.

- You need to maximize your performance by connecting with your audience of the day. This may mean dressing up for a specific meeting with senior leaders to show respect and credibility.

- This also may necessitate dressing down to become more accessible to a group of junior associates.

- You may also need to adjust your dress code based on your physical location within the company and who you see on a regular basis.

- This complexity requires an acute awareness of specific interactions of one's day.

Example 1

- You are a computer programmer. You previously have been on a quiet floor with less senior management contact, and you typically interact only with a peer group. You adhere to the corporate casual dress code.

- Now you've been moved to a new location that is on the same floor as many senior leaders. Your day-to-day peer interactions have not changed; nor have your daily responsibilities. However, you now pass many senior managers in the halls and, more importantly, they see you.

- This is your opportunity to show credibility, seriousness and respect via your appearance.

- You can adjust your professional attire just by switching out sneakers for loafers, t-shirts for collared shirts, and leaving the hoodies at home.

- This signals a professionalism that every leader wants to encourage, regardless of level or experience.

The official dress code is casual, however, in this specific situation it is advantageous to take your appearance to the next level.

Example 2:

- You are on the executive leadership committee, and you typically deal with the highest level of the company. Your dress code reflects this formality and leadership every day.

- You have a team of direct reports that you need to manage.

- In order to better connect with this group of subordinates, you start to dress more casually on Fridays, since you are typically at your desk, and this is your staff meeting day.

- Your associates now start to communicate more easily in those staff meetings, as they view you as more approachable.

- Your jeans are a significant non-verbal positive cue.

In this second example, the objective of the senior leader is to connect with his team and become more approachable as a manager. The simple act of wearing jeans and dressing down to assimilate into his team is communicating his ability to operate on the team's level. His team now thinks, "He wants to be like us and hear what we have to say."

Reality 5: Style Is Important For Your Career

Style works in many ways to:

- Reflect your industry, personality and background.
- Elevate and reinforce your credentials and priorities.
- Highlight your experiences and aspirations.
- Boost your confidence.

Your style can communicate what you want in the future, and this differs based on the individual and the industry.

As with any other type of communication, you need to be deliberate and aware of your style in order to leverage it. However, many people do not know how to describe their personal style or think that they do not have a style.

Style examples: Relaxed, professional, liberal, edgy, conservative, brand-conscious, material-conscious, whimsical, avant garde, practical.

Examples of personal style within typical industries:

Style	Industry examples
Relaxed	Computer and Information Technology
Professional	Real Estate, Financial Services
Conservative	Legal, Healthcare
Liberal	Marketing services
Edgy	Media and Communication, Art Design
Brand-conscious	Advertising
Whimsical	Education, Academics
Avant Garde	Creative Services, Art Design
Practical	Engineering and Manufacturing

In today's corporate culture, the dress code is often undefined, and it is incumbent upon each employee to determine how to dress in the workplace. Regardless of the spectrum of different personal styles, there are core tenets that guide ALL workplace styles.

Workplace style is not:

- Sloppy
- Ill-fitting
- Torn
- Dirty
- Sexy

Some people say that they do NOT have a style, and they do not care.

I would more accurately state that if you care about your career, you do care about your personal style. You just need to be aware of what you like, what signals credibility, and then learn to use it to your advantage.

The following assessment will give you the necessary information to leverage your professional image.

1. Determine your style:

Please consider the following questions to help describe your personal style. This assessment will help solidify what you like, what you need, and how to keep looking professional and appropriate.

- What do you typically wear to work?
- What would you like to wear to work?
  - What is holding you back from this? [i.e. HR policy, time, money, expertise]
- Who do you admire in your workplace because of how they look?
  - What part of their style do you like?
  - Do they wear similar things all the time?
  - Do they mix it up?
- What do you think you need to replace in your closet?
  - Specific pieces, accessories, or shoes?
- What part of your wardrobe do you rotate most often?
- If you could splurge on one item, what would it be?
- Do you ask your partner or spouse, a close friend, your family members, or a store salesperson for advice?

Whether you are starting out in your first job, rising in the ranks, or changing careers, you need to look the part. Looking the part means knowing how to build a wardrobe based on what you'll be doing most, knowing your style, and prioritizing purchases that fit those needs.

Example:

- If you are on your feet all day, make sure you have a great albeit comfortable pair of shoes that can be dressed up or down.
- If you regularly go to off-site client meetings, make sure you have a well-structured tote or bag, since you'll likely have a computer and files to carry from one site to another. You need to look organized and competent even if you are transporting an entire office with you to each client.

2. Inventory your wardrobe:

- Determine what you need in order to have a functional professional wardrobe.
- Determine what could add some fun to this wardrobe.
- Determine what needs to be tailored to your body.
- Determine what items to invest in over the next six months.
- Determine what items need to be replaced.

See Tool #1: Wardrobe Essentials 101
See Tool #2: What you have, what you need

The challenge: Figure out how to have a consistent, credible look 250 days per year without feeling overwhelmed, breaking a budget, or taking two hours to get out of the house.

3. Make everyday count (but easily):

Think about your week:

- Create a weekly plan (akin to meal-planning). Think about your meetings, events, calls, the weather, what is clean and seasonal.
- In less than five minutes, you can ensure that you're communicating confidence and credibility.

For women:

- Dresses are easy—either casual dresses or more corporate dresses. They are an entire outfit in one piece.
- Monochromatic is also an easy way to look sophisticated and ready for your day. Wearing either the same color or shades of the same color, from top to bottom and broken up with a belt or shoes, is attractive and sophisticated.
- Add a jacket. This can turn a basic, casual jeans and t-shirt into a work-savvy outfit.

For men:

- Add a pop of color somewhere unexpected, like purple socks.
- Add in a seasonal piece, like a springtime plaid in April.

In general:

- The goal is to be aware of your day and communicating the right messages with your personal presentation.
    - If you're feeling super tired, try a brightly colored shirt, scarf, or jewelry to counterbalance your mood.
    - If it is a rainy or dreary day and you're concerned about looking like a drowned rat, simply wear all black or dark clothes. It is easier to deal with the weather elements in dark colors.
- For team meeting days, new client meetings, or meetings with your boss, take it one level up by adding something that makes you feel energized.
- For regular business days, just repeat something you like and makes you feel confident.

- Casual Fridays: Jeans, yes—but you need to think about what else is going on that day. There is a tendency to automatically dress down.
  - Jeans fridays can be the toughest days—the one on which people tend to turn into sloppy messes.
- Repetition is ok. Wearing the same nice pieces is absolutely fine. Just ensure that everything is laundered, wrinkle-free, and stain-free.

Think seasons to stay appropriate and relevant:

- Dressing differently for the seasons is the easiest way to mix things up without trying too hard. Regardless of what your climate is, each season has its own color palette.
- It may be 80 degrees or 20 degrees where you live but wearing pink in April signals spring regardless of zipcode. Likewise, September and October are all about autumnal colors (yellows, reds and oranges).

4. Ask for help:

- Everyone needs help!! The "best dressed" people all have professional stylists who curate their outfits, and all of their outfits have been tailored to their specific bodies.
- Help is in a lot of different places.
  - Do not underestimate the value of talking to someone you think looks good. "I love your top; where did you get it?"
  - If you notice someone's hair, ask that person about it. That is the best type of compliment and best way to get a great contact.
  - Online services: Many sites offer stylists at every price range.
  - Pinterest: Searching can spark some outfit ideas with pieces you already own.
  - Many stores and boutiques offer personal shopping or free stylist assistance. This is a great service; they know their inventory, they know how clothes fit, and they want to help.

Real World example:

Jenny K., a New York City entrepreneur, consultant and speaker:

I definitely have a work uniform, albeit fun and trendy. I think about who is in the audience and align my outfit with the message I want to send to the audience. I'm very intentional about what I'm wearing, as I don't want to be over-dressed or under-dressed.

I have some great dresses that I wear when I am presenting or speaking to an audience. I feel confident and comfortable in these pieces. They are appropriate, fashionable and comfortable, plus they can be dressed up or down depending on where I am going for the day.

The other important consideration is how the material moves with my body, since many times I'm moving on a stage or giving a workshop and walking around a room. I do not want to be distracted by what I'm wearing. I can concentrate on my talk and audience without worrying that my outfit is wrinkled, clinging to me or being too revealing. I also never wear silk when I'm presenting, this prevents showing sweat marks.

I want to be confident and comfortable, so that I can do my job well!

Millennials comprise over 50% of the workplace and are on pace to make up 75% of the workplace over the next five years.

Bridging and transitioning both older and younger generations within in the workplace is essential to create workplace functionality.

One way that companies have embraced this generation is by loosening dress codes and letting employees decide what to wear to work. This is an easy way for people to express individuality and creativity and to assert independence.

Millennials are looking for a different experience in the workplace than previous generations, such as greater community feel and continuous personal feedback.

Millennials and younger generations want to know how and why their time and energy matters. It is not simply enough to just punch the timecard or "pay your dues" like many previous generations did without questioning the method. How this generation expresses themselves is critical, and personal style is an integral part.

Millennial Workplace Impact:

This millennial generation is forcing a change in how companies approach their workplace culture, and this directly corresponds to the workplace dress code and professional appearance.

Many people think that they should not be judged on how they look but on what they do and their attitude. However, you will be judged on everything, every day, every week, and every year:

- ✓ Your performance
- ✓ Your attitude
- ✓ Your value added
- ✓ Your appearance

Attitude is part of your professional image

Professional presence requires thoughtfulness, self-awareness, and maturity. Each person chooses how to approach her or his daily responsibilities, and this approach communicates and determines professionalism.

You can control the attitude that you bring to your job and your performance. People who have a reckless and cavalier attitude are challenging to work with and create dysfunction, even if they are high performers.

Attitude is measured in how you interact with people and how seriously you take your job.

- Attitude is communicated both verbally and non-verbally.
- Attitude is in your eye contact.
- Attitude is what you say to others.
- Attitude is your body language.
- Attitude is your professional image.

"I'm not a robot, I'm an individual": A common millennial sentiment...

Yes, you are an individual. You are an individual who works for a larger organization. You represent that organization as well as yourself. You need to strike the best balance between representing yourself and the organization. Ideally, the two converge easily.

Real World example:
The tech industry is notoriously casual, in every department, across all levels. There is only an issue when interpretations and expectations vary between management and associates.

This real-life example happens frequently, and yet there is typically little formal communication.

Kaitlyn was a dedicated and quiet computer engineer in a fast-growing data processing technology company. The company's culture was decidedly relaxed and diverse—a great improvement from her previous job in the IT department at a commercial bank. This culture appealed to Kaitlyn, as she considered herself a "non-traditional" corporate employee.

This tech company was her second job after graduating from college, and she was beginning to feel a part of this corporate community. She enjoyed her team and had started participating in the community involvement projects sponsored by the community. She liked the flexibility of the workday and ability to work remotely on some days. This corporate culture embraced independence and creativity, two aspects that Kaitlyn also valued.

This culture embraced a relaxed vibe which reflected in the dress code. People wore everything from jeans and dresses to leather jackets and sandals in the summer. Senior management wanted everyone to be comfortable and not stifled by the rigid formal dress codes of prior decades. This was a shared value and an appealing aspect for Kaitlyn.

Kaitlyn liked being comfortable at work and felt that she could focus better when comfortable, so she was getting into the habit of wearing her most casual and comfortable clothes to work. This typically entailed sweatpants and sweatshirts. She sat at her desk or in conference rooms with her team most of the day and did not think too much of this new uniform. One day, she just threw on her comfy sweatpants and running shoes. It was probably not her first choice for a work meeting, but she wanted to get to the meeting on time. Afterall, this was a casual work environment.

On this morning, Kaitlyn underestimated the traffic and ended up being about 10 minutes late to the meeting. Typically, this is not a big deal, but her director and immediate manager were at this specific meeting and everyone watched her come into the room. Only when entering the conference room with all eyes on her did Kaitlyn think that perhaps she should have dressed up a bit more, but then she moved on and joined the meeting.

After the meeting, Kaitlyn's director and her manager stayed to discuss other topics. The director asked the manager candidly, "does Kaitlyn always come to work looking like she's wearing pjs?" The manager replied after reflecting a moment, "Not always like today, but she definitely takes our casual dress code to a new level."

The director was concerned whether Kaitlyn took her role seriously enough. Due to this interaction, the director perceived Kaitlyn as more immature than he had previously thought, and he was less inclined to put her in front of other teams or external clients.

Kaitlyn will never know that her sloppy outfit communicated immaturity, and this perceived lack of experience directly impacted her corporate profile. Kaitlyn's performance was consistently above average, but the other key factors, such as professional attitude and maturity, were significantly lacking.

People do not want to believe that how they consistently present themselves can impact their career advancement. However, this non-verbal communication is very significant in shaping other's perceptions, especially the people in charge of accelerating your career.

THINK…

- How do you want to be perceived?
- Do you want to be the "sloppiest person" or the person who "takes casual to a new level in the office?"

Reality 7: How You Wear It Is Important, Too

90% of communication includes non-verbal communication.

Being aware of all your non-verbal communication, including personal appearance, can determine your professional credibility.

In addition to appearance, there are other non-verbal communication cues that signal professionalism, credibility, trust and appropriateness.

Non-Verbal Behavior	Example (s)	Importance
Facial expressions	Eye contact Smiling	Direct eye contact with colleagues is key to communicating and creating a meaningful connection.
		People who look away or do not make regular contact are perceived as insecure, unreliable or immature.
		Smiling communicates confidence, personal connection and acknowledgment.
Gestures	Firm handshakes	Firm handshakes communicate confidence, leadership and involvement.
Body language	Posture, body orientation	Facing the person speaking shows interest and respect.
		Slouching in a meeting or a presentation instantly communicates disengagement and lack of confidence.
Personal space / distance	Proximity to others in a meeting or presentation*	The amount of personal space needed when having a casual conversation with another person usually varies between 18 inches to four feet.
		The personal distance needed when speaking to a crowd of people is around 10 to 12 feet.
		When a person does not maintain this distance, it can communicate distrust, lack of professionalism and lack of credibility.
Para-linguistic	Tone, inflection, pitch and loudness	A solid, medium pitch voice is key to maintaining an audience's attention, even if the audience is one person.
		Speaking too loudly or too softly can be perceived as too aggressive or, conversely, too weak, and neither option sends a positive message.
		Do not end a sentence with an inflection, as the inflection communicates uncertainty and a lack of confidence.
Smart phone interaction	Turning phone over when a meeting starts	Smart phone interaction communicates key attributes about a person; engagement, interest, respect and self-control.
		The presenter or audience should be the priority.
		Silence phones and turn them over to signal the start of the meeting.
		If an emergency arises, then excuse yourself to take the call or text.
		Checking your phone throughout a meeting or presentation is distracting to the one conducting the meeting.
		If you need to return a call, email or text, just excuse yourself from the meeting.
		Phone etiquette can seem obvious to many people but remains a huge complaint.

*www.study-body-language.com

Only in extremely egregious situations will a manager give an associate feedback on these non-verbal behaviors. Associates will be silently judged by managers and senior executives. These senior managers make mental notes of professionalism, credibility or self-control. These metrics are often as powerful as an associate's experience or skills.

Human Resource professionals emphasize the importance of non-verbal communication when determining promotion potential and overall professional maturity.

Real World example:

I have heard dozens of stories from senior managers about the importance of non-verbal behavior and communication.

A senior HR manager at a top accounting firm related a common occurrence.

Every year, the HR team meets with each manager of every group. This is a rigorous process of evaluating each level on each team. Jeremy is the HR Director who partners with each one of the business leads to manage this process. This vigorous evaluation scores and ranks each team member based on technical skill expertise plus soft skill expertise, such as professionalism, ability to get along with others, time management skills and ability to direct a team.

Jeremy has noticed over the years of working in this technical environment that the skills that differentiate the associates on the fast-promotional track versus the associates who are slower to be promoted, are the soft skills. These are the professional skills such as leadership, communication, personal presentation and team collaboration. These are hard to quantify.

The majority of the associates brought into the organization are highly skilled at their technical skills and are focused on quantitative projects. Those who rise in the ranks are the ones with a well-rounded skill set that includes qualitative skills and non-verbal skills.

However, Jeremy notes that neither he nor anyone on the management or HR team disclose what truly differentiates one individual from another with comparable technical skills. This disclosure is considered too sensitive, subjective and not always actionable for the individuals.

The key point is that non-verbal behavior is very important, yet it is not something that managers can easily communicate to individuals. This aspect is still deemed too contentious, and it is off-limits.

The workplace has gotten very casual for many companies, and for the most part, this is a good thing. However, this casual environment can lead to many personal, albeit, unintentional pitfalls. Due to the sensitive and personal nature of these misjudgments, no one will say anything, but these are noted.

Below are a few important guides to follow.

SHORTS:

- 95% of the time you cannot wear shorts to work. This goes for women and men.
  - The other 5% of the time shorts may be acceptable when working in the creative or fashion industry.

YOGA PANTS AND SWEATPANTS:

- Yoga pants and sweatpants do not belong at the office.
- Exception: If your team is doing yoga for a charity event or team-building occasion, it would be acceptable. (Of course, this event most likely would not take place in the office.)

PAJAMAS:

- Never wear any part of pajamas to the office.
- No pajama pants or anything that resembles what one generally sleeps in should be worn in the office. No one wants to visualize you going to bed or getting up in the morning.

MANDALS or FLIP FLOPS:

- Men: NEVER wear sandals into the office. No one wants to see men's toes. Ever.
- Women: No flip flops, even if they are $350 flip flops. The noise is distracting to many people and reminiscent of the beach, not the office.

POLITICAL GARB:

- In today's intensely political environment, refrain from wearing your favorite political shirt, even on casual jeans Friday.
- Politics can distract people, harm your reputation, and bias your boss—even if you think your boss belongs to the same political party. Save it for the weekend.

RELIGIOUS GARB:

- The same rationale applied to political garb applies to religious garb. Keep your religious views separate from corporate environment.
- Save your religious garb for the weekend.

HATS:

- Do not wear hats to work unless you will be working outside or going outside.

JEWELRY THAT MAKES NOISE:

- Leave the loud bangles at home, along with any type of jewelry or adornment that makes noise.
- These noises are distracting for everyone, regardless of how fun, cute or sentimental these pieces are to you.

GLITTER or SEQUINS:

- Leave the glitter or sequins for the weekend or evening events. No exceptions.

RIPPED or TORN CLOTHES:

- Although these ripped or torn items may be fashionable and fun, the office is not the place for them.
- It is not worth the risk of being judged as sloppy or immature.

UNDERGARMENTS:

- Undergarments are meant to remain, well, under the rest of your clothes, regardless if these glimpses are intentional or unintentional.

No one needs or wants to see any signs of undershirts, underwear and/or bra straps; all major distractions.

Hygiene is HUGE

In much of my research I heard over and over the need for improved basic hygiene in the office. Nearly every person had a personal example that made a lasting negative impression.

These topics seems very basic and common sense. However, these issues exist in every office.

Hair:

- Clean hair for the office or a work meeting is essential for men and women. As one senior manager said, "dry shampoo can only be used so often." I realize that hairdressers recommend washing hair as infrequently as you can, but make sure that your hair smells ok and does not look greasy.

- If you are unsure if your hair is clean enough, then wash it.

Breath:

- Everyone drinks coffee in the morning, and everyone eats lunch at work. Just assume that you have coffee breath or lunch breath and keep gum or mints with you.

- Self-awareness goes a long way with breath. You can be the nice guy with a bowl of mints on your desk, too.

Nails & Toes:

- Clean and trimmed nails are necessary for both men and women at all times.

- Some female executives are adamant about keeping nails manicured. Manicures are not necessary, but keeping nails trimmed and clean is necessary.

- Too much adornment or garish colors on nails can be distracting. Some managers believe that nail embellishments are too juvenile, which could impact the perception of your professionalism in the office.

- If your nail polish is chipping and coming off, just take a few minutes to remove it completely. [Hint: keep acetone at your desk and just remove the polish in the bathroom if paint starts chipping mid-day]

- Men need to ensure that nails are trimmed and clean. There should be no dirt under the fingernails, regardless of how much mulching was done on a weekend.

Body Odor & Sweating:

- People often do not realize they smell. This is a challenging situation, since most adults do not intend to offend anyone.
- If you are a heavy sweater, then assume that you may smell less fresh than you would like.

DO:

- Ask someone you can trust if you smell (spouse, partner, friend, etc.)
- Wear an undershirt to prevent excess sweat from getting on your clothes
- Wear anti-perspirant and keep an extra stick in your desk drawer
- Shower everyday
- See a physician if your excessive sweating and body odor is not helped by easy interventions

DO NOT:

- Ignore the issue
- Ask your co-worker or boss if you smell unpleasant
- Wear the same clothes for work and workouts
- Skip a shower if you exercise mid-day at work
- Think that an excess of perfume or cologne will help

Eyeglasses:

- Eyeglasses are a repeated topic of annoyance for many people.
- Glasses need to be clean, straight, and not falling down your nose.
- Get a professional fitting if your glasses loosen up or get crooked. It looks ridiculous to keep pushing your glasses up on your nose.
- If you see smudges, then so does everyone else.

Clothes that Fit:

While this may seem like an obvious statement, it is one of the most distracting and unprofessional aspects of personal attire in the workplace. I heard this topic repeated over and over in my research.

The ideal is that clothes are custom made, but in reality, this is prohibitively expensive and unnecessary. However, many people need to enlist the help of a tailor, stylist or salesperson to achieve this look. Your credibility and professionalism are determined by your outward presentation.

Women:

- Aim for a comfortable fit—not too tight or too loose. If you are unsure of what a proper fit is, then ask a trusted friend, stylist, or a salesperson at a local store.
- There are many fabrics and silhouettes that are more flattering than others, so use the knowledge of a stylist or salesperson to help you.
- Invest in one pair of excellent fitting pants versus buying four that do not fit well.
- Adjust the hem of the pants, skirts or jacket sleeves if too long or too short—this is essential to look professional.

Men:

- Formal menswear is the one area in which it is most imperative to get a custom-made fit.
- You don't want to look like you are wearing your dad's shirt or stuffed into boy's pants.
- Ill-fitting dress clothes are an instant signal of distrust, lack of professionalism, and sophistication.
- Dress shirt sleeves and collar size should be measured to ensure a custom/semi-custom fit.
- Dress pants should not be too short, too long, or too big at the waist. This can be determined by the tailor or stylist.
- Suit jackets need to fit without gapping or stretching.
- Do not cinch the waist of dress pants to make them fit better.

- Do not use the last or first hole of a belt.
  - Buy either new pants and/or new belt
- Do not roll up your pants to make them shorter.
- Do not allow shirts to get so tight that the buttons are liable to pop off.

TOUGH (and sometimes unpleasant) QUESTIONS ANSWERED

1. How do you dress when working in microclimates?

- Layering is key all year around in offices. Some offices are notoriously warm, and some are super cold. This is not an excuse to walk around wearing a parka in the summer due to the A/C.

- Approach your dress based on your day; not necessarily on what you feel like wearing.

  - If you're in and out of sales calls in the summer, and it is 95 degrees outside and 65 degrees inside, then ensure you are wearing a jacket that you can easily put on and take off. Linen blazers and light-colored leather jackets are always professional options to throw over a dress or cropped pants, regardless of the office dress code.

- Invest in some layers that you can keep at your desk in case you are caught off guard for the day.

  - Wearing an old black fleece over a nice dress looks weird, and people will take you less seriously when looking like a homeless person.

  - Keep a wrap or a neutral cardigan at your desk all year round. It will be less of a distraction yet still effective to keep you warm for meetings in the arctic conference room.

2. How do you deal with sweating (both men and women)?

- Sweating is an issue that no one talks about openly in an office environment. It is an issue that most people would like to ignore, except that it is difficult to do.

- Men: wear an undershirt if you know you sweat a lot and you are in an office that is not cool enough. There are new fabrics that help in controlling sweaty underarms. Be cautious about shirt color choices. Light colors, especially blues, can be a troublesome choice, as many blue shirts show sweat much more than white or black.

- If you are perspiring on your face or forehead, keep a handkerchief or tissues in your back pocket so that you can wipe your forehead before sweat beads drip down your face. You may think that people do not notice, but they do.

- Women: Wear tops that that mask any wetness. Black poly-blend materials are often good. Light-colored cotton tops will show sweat immediately. Think about the fabrics that are used for athleisure clothing that wick sweat away from the body. You may not be able to wear Lululemon to your next presentation, but the functional aspect of those fabrics is important to remember.

  - Stay away from ALL silk shirts or dresses if you think you will be sweating. These fabrics show sweat and will dry with a salt ring staining the fabric.

- Presentations and public speaking can induce sweating, even for the person who rarely sweats. Ensure that whatever you are wearing for those occasions is sweat-proof and that you feel comfortable moving around under hot lights on a stage.

3. How can you look like you didn't just get off a plane, when you just did?

- Going straight to a work meeting from an airplane can be tricky, depending on the length of travel, the industry, and the objective of the meeting.

- Thankfully, these days, work travel uniforms have gotten much more casual. Many clothes are made with fabrics that move with your body and do not wrinkle. Additionally, they are comfortable.

- Men: Look for fabrics that say no-iron or wrinkle-resistant; most of these fabrics have a small amount of spandex woven into the wool or cotton, which adds comfort and flexibility as well as wrinkle resistance.

  - Get your shirts professional laundered. Yes, this is an additional expense, but it gives your shirts greater longevity for those traveling days, and it ensures that the collars are pressed correctly and stay in place.

- Pack an extra shirt in your carry-on case. If you are stuck on an airplane for hours in the middle of summer, a fresh shirt can make a huge difference if you're going straight to a client meeting.

■ Women: Monochromatic for travel is easy and polished regardless of the season. Leverage pieces that are very travel-friendly; many companies are making pants and tops that do not wrinkle and are comfortable.

- Travel-friendly shoes are necessary and practical when traipsing around busy airports.

- Avoid super high heels or stilettos. These options look ridiculous in an airport, and no one can walk at a decent pace in heels.

- If heels are a must, then wear a wedge or block heel or pack the heels in your carry-on bag and switch on the way to your meeting.

4. How can you look like you didn't just get out of a monsoon, when you just got caught in a monsoon?

- Nature has a way of making everyone look horrible. Traveling and commuting in nasty weather is the worst on many levels, the least of which is the way it leaves most people looking.

- Invest in weather gear: a tough umbrella, wellie boots, and a substantial raincoat with a hood.

- Try to minimize your exposure to the rain and wind by covering your work clothes up as much as possible.

- Before going to your desk, stop in the bathroom to change out of wet or sweaty gear as soon as you get to work.

5. Why does everyone care about shoes so much?

■ Shoes communicate credibility and seriousness.

- For men, in the least buy one pair of nice work shoes and wear them all the time.

- Keep shoes in good condition. Ensure that all shoes are not scuffed or worn and replace the heels when needed.

- Note: find out where the shoe repair store is in your town and use it.
- Men: Do not ever wear open-toe, Birkenstocks, or anything plastic to work.
- Women: The guidelines are less clear. Women need to ensure that all shoes are appropriate for the occasion, and women typically have more flexibility than men.
  - Leave the over 3" heels at home; these are too sexy, dramatic and distracting for the workplace. Wedges or block heels are easier to walk in and are less attention-grabbing than sky-high stilettos.
  - Leave the flip-flops, Birkenstocks, and super flimsy flats at home. Unless you are working at the Toms or Birkenstock headquarters, these are too casual.
  - If you are wearing open-toe shoes, ensure that your toes are ready to be exposed to the world.
- Ensure all shoes are in good condition—if they get too damaged, then it is time to repair or replace.

6. Can I wear my favorite holiday sweater to the office?

- Dressing for a holiday season can be appropriate for the office but dressing like you're going to a costume party is not.
- Unless you have an official "ugly Christmas sweater" party or you work in a preschool, leave the whimsical clothing for the weekend.
- What is whimsical clothing?
  - Christmas or Hanukah sweaters, jingle bell earrings, giant holiday ties, bunny ear headbands, light up necklaces, skeleton t-shirts, Santa Claus hats...
- Dressing for the season or a holiday entails reflecting color choices with the current season—this IS a great thing.
  - Do: wear seasonal colors in the corresponding seasons; i.e. autumnal colors in the fall—oranges, dark reds and flannels in the fall months are appropriate and encouraged. Also, it is refreshing to see pops of spring colors in the springtime.

- Do: wear plaids around the holidays
- Don't: wear jingle bell earrings or Santa hats to meetings
- Don't: wear anything that lights up on your body
- For men, it is acceptable to show festive spirit via your socks: Santa, shamrocks, and Easter eggs are a subtle way to participate in holidays without looking like you're trying to win a prize for best costume.

7. Do I really need to iron or launder my dress shirts?

- YES, YES, YES.
  - Wrinkles on shirts are super distracting on both men AND women—it makes it look like you slept in your clothes and do not care about yourself.
  - Either steam, iron or launder your shirts.

8. Do I need to alter my clothes?

- If your pants, shirts, jackets are too big or too small, then YES, YES, YES.
- Wearing ill-fitting clothes makes you look like you are an orphan child and that you do not care about yourself or your job. If something is too big or too small, it is noticeable and distracting.
- This issue is more significant for men in a professional dress environment: the neck, sleeve and waists need to precisely fit the body. This shows you care about details and professionalism.
- Investing in a good tailor is huge for your professionalism and your confidence—you will feel better when your clothes fit you.
- Everyone gains or loses weight, and this is not a big deal, but your clothes need to accommodate these personal changes.
  - If this means maintaining pants and shirts in varying sizes, then that is ok. Losing or gaining weight is not an excuse to look sloppy or unprofessional.

9. How do I find a suitable alternative for jeans on "jeans Friday?" I do not like wearing jeans to work.

- If you do not feel good in jeans, then definitely do not wear jeans! There are plenty of alternatives that allow you to participate in casual Friday and not look like you're above everyone else by dressing more formally.

- Ideas: For women, add a denim jacket or chambray shirt to black pants. Wear corduroy pants in the winter and linen pants in the summer. Your shoes will also signal your level of dressiness. You can don your more casual shoes on these days, too.

- For men, you can opt for khaki jeans or just more casual khakis and a casual button-down.

- Invest in a nice pair of jeans that are good for work; these tend to be darker, and they should fit well and not be torn. Leave the 10-year-old jeans at home for cleaning out the garage.

10. How much exposed skin is ok?

- Guidelines: If you think you're showing too much skin, you probably are. Err on the side of showing less skin. Women can appropriately show more a bit more skin than men in the office.

- Women:
  - Do: consider your industry and the occasion. What is advantageous in one industry may be not in another.
  - Do: ensure that your toes and feet are groomed if you are showing them in sandals.
  - Do: shave your legs and underarms if you plan to have bare legs and wear sleeveless tops.
  - Do: make sure your skirts and dresses are long enough to cross your legs and not ride up your thigh while walking, sitting or standing.
  - Do: wear skirts that cover at least ¾ of your thigh.
  - Do: make sure your clothes cover your undergarments.
  - Do NOT: show your midriff.
  - Do NOT: show cleavage.

- Men:
  - Do: show your forearms only.
  - Don't: show your shoulders, midriff, ankles or toes. No one wants to see any of those body parts in the office.
  - Don't: wear mandals (man-sandals).

11. Can men wear short sleeve shirts in the office?

- Yes, short sleeves are acceptable in all dress codes, except for a formal business environment.
- If you need to wear a tie, then pair your tie with a long-sleeved shirt.

12. Can I wear perfume and cologne to the office?

- Err on the side of too little perfume or cologne. Office space is shared space, and not everyone finds your perfume or cologne to be as pleasantly aromatic as you do.
- Many people also have allergies, and certain perfumes and colognes can exacerbate these allergies.
- You do not want to be known as the person who wears too much perfume or cologne—this is an instant way to lose credibility in the office.

13. Can I expose my body ink (i.e. tattoos)?

You need to know your environment in order to successfully answer this question.

- Traditional/Conservative: Banking, finance, law, real estate, medical, large corporate entities
  - Traditional guideline: do not show tattoos
- Non-traditional/Liberal: Academia, creative/design, culinary, entertainment, construction
  - Modern guideline: if you work in a liberal atmosphere, exposing your tattoos is acceptable and can be advantageous. The tricky part is truly knowing your environment.

14. What is the big fuss about facial hair and beards?

- Facial hair and beards need to be clean and groomed just like the hair on the head. With good hygiene, facial hair and beards are completely acceptable for any industry, with any level of dress code.

15. Do I need to dress up for a video conference or Skype session?

- You need to mimic the level of dress in the office. If it is a weekday and you would normally wear a suit, then you should be dressed to that same level (suit pants without the coat).

- If you are doing a video conference on a weekend, then this dress code shifts, and you can wear what you would typically wear on a weekend—a much more casual vibe.

- Note: Virtual office dynamics add a complicating aspect into your dress code—you have less ability to see others in the office, less opportunity to learn by example, and less opportunity to determine what is advantageous for your personal appearance.

- Ensure you communicate with your colleagues and/or boss to make sure you have the appropriate attire when you visit the office and have corporate meetings or virtual meetings.

16. Do you dress for your current level or the level you hope to achieve?

- Answer: It depends

- This is the pitfall that most people fall into. Some try too hard and look out of place, and others do not differentiate themselves enough.

- You need to be aware of what the top people in the office wear and dress to that level when you interact with them.

  - Elevate your look on certain occasions, like a formal presentation or large meeting where you will be viewed by lots of people.

  - If your office or desk is within close proximity to senior management, it can be advantageous to dress to their level more frequently. This management may not be in your everyday work life, but they certainly see others in the office. Your professional attire may be the only communication you have with senior management.

17. Can I wear my "luxury" brands to the office?

- This is a tricky topic and really depends on your industry, department and level of management.

- A basic guideline is that one statement or luxury piece is the maximum; i.e. Gucci loafers, Louis Vuitton bag, Tory Burch earrings, etc.

- One piece goes a long way and you do not want to look like a Nascar outfit.

- Luxury pieces can be polarizing in many offices. They can be perceived as showy and ostentatious, and some people may think that you really do not need the job if you can afford a $400 belt.

- Contrarily, in some industries, like fashion, design, and real estate, luxury clothing pieces are acceptable and communicate a level of success.

- Again, knowing the type of environment you work in is critical, so err on the side of "less is more" with luxury pieces.

18. Can I wear shorts to work?

- No, 95% of the time; the other 5% is for the people working in fashion or creative industries.

- No shorts for anyone working in a traditional office.

TOOL #1: WARDROBE ESSENTIALS 101

Professional wardrobe:

Below please see the foundational and timeless pieces that most corporate men and women need.

MUST HAVE TIMELESS PIECES

Women:
Black suit: well-fitting—can be worn as separates

Blouse: dressed up or down, stain-free, wrinkle-free

Neutral heels and neutral flats

Large, structured handbag

Nice jeans

Men:
Dark suit: well-fitting

Dress shirts: well-fitting, laundered, stain-free

Dress shoes: clean and maintained

Work bag: messenger bag, backpack (not one that you take hiking)

These seem like no-brainers, but many people do not have these professional pieces that signal credibility and maturity. These are the items that need to be maintained year after year, regardless of your industry. Even in the super-casual tech industry, these items can be leveraged on their own to create a fun, hip and appropriate style.

Casual wardrobe 101:

Many of the professional wardrobe pieces will work in a casual setting when paired with casual pieces.

However, there are a few caveats:

- No suit
- No conservative dress shoes

You will need other key pieces:

- Jean, jeans, jeans
- Casual shoes: loafers, booties, wedges, "fancy" sneakers
- Layering pieces (weather- and season-dependent): jackets, vests.

INVESTMENT PIECES:

- Investment pieces are classic, basic pieces that transition from season to season and remain relevant year after year, despite fashion trends or dress codes.
- Classic example: trench coat or leather coat
- Curate these important pieces over time, as these pieces will cost you more per item but will last for literally over a decade.
- With investment pieces, think *less is more*. Buy one pair of great fitting black pants that may cost more but that you will wear time and time again, year after year.

Women:
Black jacket
Trench coat
Black trousers
Black and tan heels (any height)

Men:
Overcoat
Trench coat
Leather messenger bag
Sport coat
Loafers

ROTATE FREQUENTLY:

- Depending on your personal style, budget and workplace, lean into accessories to show your personality, trends, and changes of season.
- Accessories are an economical way to add interest to your wardrobe.

Women: Scarves, jewelry, belts, shoes

Men: Belts, socks, sport coats

TOOL #2: Professional Attire Inventory:

What You Have, What You Need

Determine the ideal outfit and then think about what you currently have for this situation.

Determine any gaps or missing pieces that exist in your current wardrobe.

1. Interview:

Ideal:

Currently in your closet:

Gaps:

2. Every day:

Ideal:

Currently in your closet:

Gaps:

3. Travel:

Ideal:

Currently in your closet:

Gaps:

4. Presentation:

Ideal:

Currently in your closet:

Gaps:

5. Off-site meeting:

Ideal:

Currently in your closet:

Gaps:

List all pieces that are missing in your wardrobe.

Prioritize these pieces based on necessity and cost.

Determine what pieces are investment pieces (over $500).

NOTE: For every item purchased, one item must be donated or sold.

This item is something that: (1) does not fit, (2) has a stain or hole, and/or (3) has not been worn in a year.

Acknowledgements

Thank you to the many people all over the country that gave their time, candid perspectives, insights and support for this book. These interviews and research helped me develop an authentic and robust guide. I am so grateful for their generosity.

I also want to thank my patient husband, Casey, three energetic boys, David, Henry & Philip, plus my furry writing partner, Millie. Their unwavering support and encouragement were instrumental in helping me complete this guide and launch Code of Clothes.

About the Author

Elizabeth Jones is the founder and CEO of Code of Clothes LLC. Beth has more than 20 years of business experience in Fortune 500 corporations, working in marketing and change management. Beth has seen the power of personal presentation on many levels, from entry-level positions to CEOs.

Beth earned a BA from Georgetown University, an MBA from Vanderbilt University and attended the University of Sussex through the Study Abroad Program. Beth lives in Cincinnati, Ohio.